Nailed

to the

Sky

M. Anne Sweet

a *gazoobi tales* book
Seattle, 2003

Nailed to the Sky
a *gazoobi tales* book

All rights reserved. Printed in USA.
Copyright © 2003 by M. Anne Sweet.

*Some of these poems have been published under the
same title by Linear Arts Books, Sconset, MA*

For information address:
gazoobi tales
p.o.b. 12651
Everett, WA 98206
or
gazoobi@gte.net

ISBN 0-9679364-1-1

Library of Congress Control Number: 2003108259

book design by Thomas Hubbard
10 9 8 7 6 5 4 3 2 1
first edition

Credits

The author would like to thank the editors of the following anthologies and journals in which many of the poems in this volume first appeared:

A Wise Woman's Garden, Aleutian Goose Festival Poetry Contest Anthology of Winners and Finalists, The Apricorn Anthology, Barefoot Grass Journal, Coast Weekend, The Charlotte Poetry Review, Chrysanthemum, Crab Creek Review, Dream Machinery, Equine Image, Main Street Rag Poetry Journal, PoetsWest Literary Journal, Pontoon, The Raven Chronicles, The Seattle Five Plus One Poetry (Pig Iron Press), Talking Raven, Washington Thoroughbred and the following online journals: The Green Tricycle, The Horsethief's Journal, Pif Magazine and Switched-on Gutenberg. Also, my thanks to Art Fusion at Habitude and The People's Theatre.

Author's Acknowledgments

I would like to thank all of the writers and artists I have been fortunate to come in contact with through the years, for each of them has left an indelible mark.

In particular I thank Irene Drennan, Crow Sister, who taught me the "music" of poetry and with whom I have at times connected on an unspoken level; and Jack Remick, who with unwavering support taught me the power of metaphor, the crunched image and digging deeper.

I offer my humble thanks to Priscilla Long, for writing the introduction to this book and for her insightful and in-depth critiques over the years; and to publisher Thomas Hubbard for his belief in the book, for his patience and gentle guidance and for his attention to "getting it right."

There have been others, writers and non-writers alike, who have also touched me on a soul level in large and small ways. It is impossible to name them all, but I would like to mention poet, artist and shaman John Stehman; poets Kevin Coyne and Raymond Greotte (John Raven); and performance poet Bart Baxter, to whom I have looked as a model for presenting poetry powerfully and effectively in the oral tradition.

And these most precious gifts cannot go without mention: friend, abakuá and collaborator, artist and musician Chuck Smart, who in the sharing of his vision has both supported and increased my vision; artist and friend Melanie Anderson; dressage instructor and friend Jim DiMilte; my parents, John and Mo Sweet, and siblings, Patty, Jack, Bob, Tom and Tim; and, of course, my partner and soul mate George C. Hopkins III, who has given me generous amounts of space and support for my creative endeavours as well as a critical ear at times.

Last, but not least, I dedicate this book to Jo Nelson (1946-2001), Crow Sister, mentor and peer, friend and guide, Yemayá.

Introduction

Anne Sweet's poems burn, bite, claw, curse, and howl. They are "dressed in black widows and pain," they "drool venom," their "horse wild hooves fly." And they sing:

> When bear lumber from caves
> yellow breasted birds chick
> in the dee dee sun.
> Frogs cough in a pond
> phlegm thick with croak.

Sweet's poems are musical, but also visual. These are painterly poems, wrought with a palette of hot oranges, reds, and yellows. The crows in "Eclipse" sit "black/beads on pumpkins." The river in "Snake River" "runs red with salmon." A letter reporting the results of a mammogram bears "oranges and pears sent/from a place in the sun." No prosy-gray lines here.

It is always revealing to ask how a poem moves. How does it get from here to there? Is there a narrative engine, a story driving it home, or does it move by associative leaps? Is the poem a collage, with layers and colors, or a horse race, galloping syllables? To move is to act, so the question can be put another way: What act does the poem perform? Again and again, Sweet's poems move, shift, mutate by means of alchemy — the mixing and cooking of disparate elements. The poems perform acts of fusion — the human world fuses with the natural world, the physical with the spiritual, outside with inside, infinitesimal with infinity. The silver bulb of a spider becomes a planet, her webline leaves starprints. A woman menstruating in the ancient sacred house, separate from men, becomes Mt. St. Helens. The volcanic mountain cramps, her belly caves, she bleeds hot lava.

Sweet's sensibility is imagist. Her themes — the life of a woman; the interweaving of animal, plant, and human life; the creation of art — often shape-shift themselves into the form of an archetypal figure — from crone-crow to chorus girl to a certain missing Zap Pow hero. We are here in the presence of the blood, bone, and essential stardust that make up the cosmos, not excluding fuschia lipstick, guitar twangs, and stiletto heels.

What is the poet's method? How does she work? She reveals her technique in a poem titled "Crossing Thresholds": "I have flame-tangled lightning-set words/and spat them out,/fragile pennings that burn my fingers." So.

For five years during the 1990s, I workshopped and performed with Anne Sweet in the group of poets The Seattle Five Plus One. We six very different poets stimulated and challenged each other, worked our butts off, and drew a loyal and much appreciated audience to our readings. Poetry makes for glorious occasions and happy times! Anne Sweet has continued to develop her art within a number of contexts and venues. It honors me greatly to invite you now to turn the page, to taste these poems. They are delicious.

Priscilla Long
Poet and author of
Where the Sun Never Shines,
A History of America's Bloody Coal Industry

Nailed
to the
Sky

M. Anne Sweet

Contents

Nailed to the Sky

A Room
of
Dark
Women

Three Sisters of the Crow

Crow crone dips in the iron
pool of sister eyes
and crosses sweet river of reed.
Thistles plucked
drift into the float downstream.

Owl brother hunts silence into dusk.
His yellow bladed beak
pierces robin's blood breast.
Raven mourns
the coffin winter rakes over him.

Hag crow with cracked jaw,
constant sister of the tell all,
roosts on the bank
of her black forgiveness.
Hunched half-moon into belly folds
she drinks winter's brown fog.

Twilight sister calls,
Follow, follow.
Our bird blessings
water the silent soil,
fallow fragments of rock and bone.

In thickets of no light
crow sisters tip their heads
and sing through blue throats.
Sky teeters on their vacant call.

Search for the Black Madonna
For women in Bosnia, India and Rwanda

Madonna
mother of child
you tell me
step into the dark
and in the black silent
in the hymn-laden oh holy night
lies a Muslim stabbed
by the Serb's brown cock.

White and safe I
while this brown woman
will bear a child with no home
will not name it
will leave it
it the pronoun of her denial
to herself
to her husband
to her father's father.

Her husband
who will cry angry at her
left with the scar of a child
a child whose father came
and left at the same moment
a child born from a pelvis
driven hard through.

Madonna, you tell me
sit with the dark
and in the stone white darkness
faces surround me
the faces of cherub-faced Madonnas
whose babies are boy.
Come into the light
the light of a crucifix
fire warm on your face.

This crucifix is woman.
In the deep cavern of India
her black face not painted
not stone
in her womb is not boy.

Brideslave holds in her water
what her husband disdains
the ultrasound visage
of a tiny self suckling the sorrow
of her mother's heart.
Brown bosom stained by acid tears
her colostrum sours
her cataracts grow thick.

Madonna, I stepped into the dark
into a room of dark women.
The darkness is pure and ancient.

Chorus Line

Chorus girls bob beatwise,
dark-haired,
arm pit to arm pit,
in long-legged lines,
all the same namelessness
built up in their faces.
Their cast iron consciousness,
eighteen all-legs-one
catapult my daydreams sideways.
I do not try to escape.
I try to think their samethoughts,
their Catholic school girlthoughts,
but my rough edges
scrape at their bare thighs.
I bow apologetic genuflections
and wish I had not touched them.
Martyred stillborn children
are they real?
or wind-up representations
of coalesced fragments
of the massive oneness of us all?
If for only just one misstep
I could count the separate beats
of their heartthrobs.

Stiletto-heeled women,
they have kept to themselves
in their own same way.
It is the way each their dust has settled
that makes them whole
and alone.
Dust finds all the small differences.
I lean close
and carefully
do not breathe it away.

Shamanic Eye Echoes

In Montana
I find arrowheads,
stone and earthsmell.
I remember a shaman's eyes.

Out of his eyes
beaver flow from dams
and the cave mouth
of his elk mother
breathes out brotherson,
swallows daughterfather.
Nostrils snort disease
tread in on boot heels.

Pox blankets snowwarm
wrap white
the wings of geese.
Parchment lips
search for buffalo water,
cough blood,
blow in the wind.

Beaded in shell and onyx
his magic rustles,
caught in the throat of fall.
He spits out songs
stripped of bark.

When I see
his eyes empty in me
he speaks cliff edged
to sky.
Wolf, his dog guide,
hollow howl opens the night.

Step for the Stars

Tethered   untethered
adrift where black velours my face
a spider   silver bulb with platinum legs
Runs its webline   leaving starprints.
Her hairy tongue on my cheek says
she will bite off my head
lay her eggs in my chest
the hot blood of our mating
she incubus   I incubate
her young feed on my heart   my lungs
fill with their gas   ignite from sparks
when asteroids collide   my skin
unwinds in fine tendrils.
I stretch my single cells
end to end
blood to bone
I am infinite   and white.
Silver she orb
waits to bite off the head
of her dying mate
dark planet drooling bile.

Inside Pleiades

Dressed in black widows and pain,
sulfur yellow heat splits my leg.
Seeds spill sterile on brick.
My pen, fountain tipped,
razors its line through my buttock,
down thigh and calf,
hot branding my sole with ellipsis,
the clucking of old women,
hysteric voices raised pitch upon pitch.
My back their metate,
they grind my thoughts to dust.
Their ragged teeth snap when I bend.

Tongue-tied   delirious   I dream
grey and white
of sleep on ice   and mist.
I float through forests of stone.
My canoe scrapes
the rock shore   I step
under clouds   sun thin   footsteps
squeezed out of sand
follow grey foam   the creep
and curve of ocean waves.

Seagulls eat from my hand
meager shells   words wirespun
galleys of crusted bread.
They feed me
waterworn drifts and alabaster flights
through mother of pearl
to an earth wall
green and blue with macaws.
Wing red shatters my grey.

The Night of the
Seattle Five Plus One Minus Me Reading
at the Roadrunner Coffeehouse and Coyote Comics

The night my turtle,
white ninja truck,
stopped swimming
the black pond pavement,
Coyote grins, guzzles toads
from the tank of my want
to go and go,
leaves me to shrivel,
desert kill in light that kisses my forehead red,
kisses my ankles through burned socks,
kisses the smile pasted moon I expose.

Turtle prey, hard shell hides the soft
my flesh pours into poems.
Stuck without wheels,
without wings,
unable to leap tall buildings,
single bound,
I sing my song
a one-word poem the pitch of fire engines.

Where is my Zap Pow hero
blue cape muscled red S smacking my lips?
Where is that masked man,
my silver Kemosabe?

Hi ho,
Coyote laughs.
Poems spill from viper jaws
to the empty chairs of my house
and to dogs that howl when sirens wail.

Sky Pony

Icicles freeze
the prairie mane of a storm,
trees bridled in white.
Hooves paw silver against greyblue.

I weave a braid of hair,
knot, unknot
the barren days,
spinning wheel echoes
bend me
under a sky tone-deaf.
Smoke chimneys
in the back up wind,
smoke of a husband pipe
randy for spring.

When bear lumber from caves,
yellow-breasted birds chick
in the dee dee sun,
frogs cough in a pond
phlegm thick with croak.

My wintered hand on dry ground,
I ask for rain.
Rain comes,
I ask for sun.
But again the black sky colics,
cows hunch against
the pony wind.

Steel String Dream

The guitar speaks through the blue haze
twang echo of forgiven dreams
slung low across the night.
Time is stripped from bone
where callous midnight hugs me
and cares not that this is rape.

The steel edged twang
laps at my throat and howls
 Pray to me, inhale sulfur,
 lay my burning string across your palm.
 Strip the clothes from your breast,
 feed me your heart bound in ribs of glass.
Night forbids my broken cry.
My chest flesh opens.
Red wine welts my arms
and my soul uncharted chants
night sweat dreams,
wind chimes swept to sea.

Desert Wane

Hell was my home
salt hills crossed by trails
of life spent hollows
barb wire torn land
crows blacktop bound
scavenge rockseed spilled
from the father sack.

Powder fell from my face
in soot lines   canyons
I locked myself in
skin crust calluses
split tight and hard
from desert rain
scar mounds
sweet belladonna silents.

Crows clack wind words
their hot white caws
tongue my ear
scrape the crust from my skin.

A tap root digs
through fossils petrified and wood
waters my sleep
white veins coiling through shale.
The sun sucks my neck
pulls my green cap
through mounds I blossom
white-hot diva.

Conductor

Red eye tired,
bound to a train I can never get off,
memories fade
like the old upholstered fabric
of this train I ride and ride.

Every green-eyed station wench
and all the green-eyed forests
stir in my diary the scent of pine,
while on each long walk
my eyes burn
through the grey of the smoking car,
through the stale breath
of thick-curtained sleeping compartments,
through day cars and yellowed lavatories
wet with the water of sponge baths.

At night between towns
demons lure me in sleep
to walk the narrow couplings between cars.
Bell towers toll.
Someone else's voice in a dream cries,
All aboard!

Park Walk: A Vignette

Above the movie marquee
seagulls arc and twist
on the doveless wind.
Sunset dries the horizon
in front of park benches
where couples, nickel-skinned,
steam heat the cool air.
Bonfires die in embers
of drift-split wood.

An old man stands,
a tight-lipped rock wall
banked against grey.
He curses the phrases of sea waves,
the bowed wings of gulls,
a cormorant staccato against red.
He rages Bruch's violin
g minor concerto
for his wife breathless,
her cold hands stiff.
Clutched in her talon feet,
he pulls night
around the wounds he flays.

Keeper of the Sunset

She weaves the webs of spiders
between her toes.
The mound of her chest,
a mountain snowdraped with down,
her shoulders round into foothills
of smoke plumes.
The Aleutian stretch of her black neck
blushes white on her cheek.

She wades in marsh grass,
a chatter of beak in cool water, she dips
and drinks with head tipped back.
She pads across tundra moss,
yawns open her wings,
folds and settles on squat legs.

Her head tilts, her ebon eye
searches the pottered sky,
sleek and slate grey,
listens for the thrub
of wing beats riding a draft,
tumbling tier to tier
to rest on the stroke and pull of flight.

In her memory, honks flock
the pulse and flow of her heart,
louder, then louder
till she stands, honking back
at a V-wing of black
scrimshawed in a glaze of vermilion sky.

The Barmaid's Story
For Anita Hill

I.

Alc flowed free in steins,
innuendoes honey thick
on her half-bare breasts.

She told of a prince.
From his mouth popped a fish.
His purple heart enraptured her.

The pythons stirred
                    hissed.
They saw her honeyed breasts bare,
appled.
They did not recall
the sunrise in her eyes.

She spoke all day his words,
silver-skinned words that smelled.
His purple heart enraptured her.

They emptied their steins,
clawed at her apple breasts,
licked apple flesh from their nails,
asked why
his purple heart enraptured her.

She couldn't say why –
he was a prince that smelled
of silver-skinned fish.

II.

Her eyes
the sunrise he saw
when he surfaced
to feed on flies
above the slippery waves

his prey the flies.
He the prey of eagles
a feather floats
from passion lofted.
He drowns in the mundane
he seeks to crush
with untruths
vulgar stories of rape gone bad.

Eagle man reaches inside Eagle woman
the barmaid virgin he kissed
silver lipped
behind closed doors
no one to confirm or deny
the fishery of sliming
through wet reaches of conspiracy.
He blinded her with stars
silver skin reflected.
She wrote angled stories
of deeds bent on raising
the eyebrows of his peers
while he hid behind rock
caressing her applehoney breasts.

The day she told
he leapt from surface water
eyes blazing the truth sunhot.
His purple heart.
She enraptured
by deeds hidden in kelp.
Eagles mate
their plunging ritual ends
a breath above the blue water
tumble to triumph
feathers fall to his reach
like flies at dusk.
His airborne leaps touch only
the lips of her sunrise eyes
his fakery not the victim
he preyed for.

The Evidence Suggests

**"... that moments of depression were followed by
moments of creativity ... the effort was considerable
and the balance ... was a fine one."**

— From *Virginia Woolf: A Biography,* by Quentin Bell

Nightshade,
poison buds on your berry lips,
chameleon hidden
among blackberry and ivy,
your wicked fingers entwined
in holly and bush fuchsia,
your taste thick
in my dead goose's throat.

Purple bells ring on dagger hands,
sharp-edged finger curls beckon me
down vines I hand over hand
past sticker and bee sting.
Stalking the dark and dirty webroot,
I yank at the stale green smell of death.

Virginia,
poison-coated stamen bloom on your cheeks.
Flowers purple with yellow teeth,
semen to seed, their red heads bolt.
You pluck berries,
nightshade among holly,
swallow their red hot sap.

Shade entwines your throat,
your gums pale, your skin ash grey.
Bitter arsenic laps your blood white nectar,
entangles your feathers in vine.

CRaZY
An overture and fugue in three voices

Overture

After the 'quake they swore
there was nothing deeper
than the cracked pavement it raised.
I believed there was more.
I read late into the night
in pink feathered pajamas.

On wings I travel.
A jayhawk swoops.
Black-eyed geese
raise the wind with their wings,
fold them, white against warm,
call me to open the barn door.

Fugue

I arrive at the market
hidden in brown robes
carried on the arms of animals
set down wild in the square
on my search for a crocodile
that will live
in the pond behind my adobe.

    She came in on wings of the white swan
    summoned us
    through eyes that saw us
    centuries before.
    We came through dust
    desert risen from hooves.

      That crazy woman
      lives out there with those animals
      never talks

has that glass-eyed look.
She's crazy, I tell you
comes to town on a camel
or wild boar!
Hair stringy
never bathes
or does, but lord knows how or when.

They think she is crazy.
We care only
that she thinks as we think
and the crying we hear
stops us prick-eared.
She laid before us
the end of the river.

Their shadows speak
I am the crazy woman
broad brazen woman
my dreams   feral animals
I am the crazy woman.
I live in the forest
evergreen
surrounded by walls
stone minds.

It's no wonder she doesn't talk
lives with those animals, their smell
the gag madness of noise   dust   dung
senseless up to her knees
the forest
all that dung.
And those swans come and go
shadows that give you chills
look up
and there they go
back to that crazy woman.

We brought her above trees
to the place we found in her mind
set her cradled down
nested in feathers.
She awakes in silence
surrounded by beasts.
Wild noises she hears
blend with voices
from rocks   the trees.

I am the crazy woman
hiding from bruises of town sound.
I travel mountains and rocks
in search of silence speakers.
Dawn, the dusk halflight
allows translation
without language we speak.
At night the angels of cat slaves
welcome me.

We see what she sees
hear the voice of her wants.
She reads us with twitches
the town people fear.
The day she markets
we lie beside her.
She mounts   us-one
the twitching stops
we breathe with one breath
through the morning grey fog.

She comes every week
that crazy woman
never speaks
wanders and looks
picks up apples, bananas, kiwi
woven goods of the miller's wife
runs her hand through his grain.
We watch her go   stand to stand

tried small talk   now we just smile and nod.
She's crazy, that wild stringy hair
and who knows what she'll ride in on.

I am the crazy woman
surrounded by dust
the smoke of animals
their desert roam
the forest I built them.
They find what they need.
I suck on the life they live
water lifted by white swans
bottled from the river I am.

It's like a carnival
we've all come to watch.
That crazy woman
boys taunt her
some drunk son of a bitch
once tried to drag her behind that far stall
planned to have his way with her
came back looking like
he'd seen hell's furies
never saw her again that day
and he wouldn't speak of it
just walked out of town
and never came back.

Unflinching
we feel road stones
thrown by boyish fears.
They think she is crazy,
she   the sublime rhythm
dust
the breathless sky
above dry lake beds,
a town empty of water,
crazy with thirst.

Mizu's Mask

She names herself water
and green mountain.
Beads and coarse string skew gold lamé,
her face in odd angles.
She buttons her eyes with gold coins.
Her grandfather's clay fills her mouth.

She says
Grandfather, unmask your face.
Behind your horns and red eyes –
a grass pasture.
Behind your mouth parched
by volcano wind a streambed winds.
Your sigh binds my feet.
The stone in your gut cuts my soles.
She pats the yarn of his black hair.
Hunger snarls her lace.

She sorts pictures and maps,
puzzles and rust leaves
wedged in blank pages.
His flute sound flows from her heart.

Ferns unfurl in layers of clay.
She rakes guarded lines,
sand around black river rock.
She names herself water
and green mountain.

Ilwaco

The bagpipe wind whistles,
its full breath discord rasps sand
from basalt cliff, each grain
grandfathered by each grain.
This mute tongue has tasted
the underbelly of pelican,
the belly of gull   kites unstrung
and shell. It licks me,
porous air ancients rough my skin.

At cliffbase, among sea ropes of kelp,
shorebirds dance the tide flats.
Long needle pine root in black sand.
Inside a drift log wigwam,
in a chorale of windpipe and timpani,
sunshafts stain the glass sand gold.
I tithe my naked sweat, thin offering
on an altar of drifts decades deep.

Would you call that plagiarism?

you asked.
Here are her words
for you to use,
her writings, handed to me,
corner worn
and frayed at the spine.
On brittle pages I answer.

Would I bathe downstream
as she bathes, pat on powder
she washes away, scent myself
with oil from her skin?
Her eau de cologne sits
on your memory shelf.
I will bottle myself here
beside her, within reach
of your hand, perhaps crack her lid
that air may take her away.

I hunt my words in the fireflow,
distill their fat with my flame.
My candle draws you,
snow white moth,
feather me with wingdust.

White Girl Jive

I dig black girl jivetalk.
Holy silent, I enter their heat,
their granddaddy hallelujahs,
getdown gospel eddies,
cool, cool lava in beatrun flow.

Robes hang from their drum speak
in red-yellow spirit dance,
mask echoes carved through layers
tongue cut by song chant
they peel off muscle and skin.

Black girls sing the marrow from bone,
soften it with their teeth
and birdfeed my mouth.
Their beat fills my craw.

Marian Anderson

At the feet of Abraham, clouds of doves,
their bright E flats and low Ds,
velvet the marbled crowd.
The long shadow of your voice
feathers the wind
with liquid petals of pansy and peony.

Black pigeon in a nest of white stone,
your dark contralto parts an ocean
of charcoal midnights.
Ivory voices your strings,
your sharps and flats,
the honey of your burnt molasses.

Evening Star
For Georgia O'Keeffe

In Stieglitz' glass eye, she erupts
yellow against the black and umber sky,
in red leaf and white cliff.

She opens my skin on her canvas.
Water colours my cheek with her stroke,
blue stamen   sand
in my hair and under my nails
a train steams half circles of grey.
Light billows my plain,
my pulse lunges   russet burls
unfurl from buffalo bones.
I stretch her iris horizon,
her black hills without shade.

Carmina Islandia
A Song to Myself

Mirabel, bury me
in the white sand off the coast
of your peppered skin.
The sun has dotted your eyes with freckles.
Blonde seaweed grows from your skull.
A rock cave enters the between
below your breasts
where seagulls float your updraft.

Wave lather lips your cave,
circles the edge of your lagoon,
your catttailed wetlands.
You sing the redwing's song in granite grains
on a sandbar where I lie
buried beneath your notefall.

Capistrano

In France, I'm told,
if a swallow falls from the sky,
legs too short
for wings longing flight,
one must lift it in cloth hands
like this year's crow
fallen from first glide.

For two days under hovering caws
that warned you away,
you lifted and tossed the young crow.
You fed it worms,
worried over scent-tainted wings.
Then one day its fledgling flight held the air.

I have slept above the touch of ground,
taken insects on wing with eyes sonar sharp.
You and I have mated on currents of air.
In our passion I fell, your scent on my wings.
My legs grew short,
I flapped for loft mute air denied me.

Gather me in cloth and toss.
In a stream of wind I will leap on sleek wings.
Your cords of light bind and release me,
release and bind me.
With mud and saliva,
again and again
I nest in your mission eaves.

Violin

I am master only of the skewed rows of purple iris
at the moment I plant them.
Thread follows a needle
through a silk sleeve.
Violin,
tears drip from your strings.

When art has found its breath
in the hand of the artisan
the hoax most cruel is this:
When applied to canvas
winter melts.
Violin,
touch one single snowflake
wet to my cheek
and I will sing you iris dancing.

The taste of power fades
in the robes of concubines.
Their pinings lick seductive
at the navels of mongrel kings
who retch the poet's plumes of conceit.

Violin,
cement laden hearts crack
when your melody lands.
I crave the words
that open the throats of mannequins
and turn papier-maché faces to flesh.

Blood

Snake River

The river runs red with salmon.
My river runs red,
fertile drops that spread
through a tapestry of months.

Snake River telescoped reveals
a swim upstream against backwash,
the leaps,
the eyes tearless,
the noises of so few
unheard.
This year the count of one male
and one female
draws a bead through the gun sight of my mind.

So many eggs spawned,
washed downstream.
Whispery are the thoughts I cancel
that this is
may be
the last run of salmon
through the mouth of my stream.

Mammogram

"We compress because we care."
> — Sign in the radiologist's office

Waist-naked
against machine cold
the tech warm-handed arranges
flesh of my fear
flesh scared answer
that poison lumps have eaten
the flesh of my youth,
mammaries for babes
I have not yet had.
What if they arrive to lakes empty,
rivers dry,
wild game fled south
when fungus tainted leaves
twist and turn brown
in the no rain sun?

Year to year
my flesh spread
passion bruised
suckled between plates
counting the times teeth
hard and white
have sunk into brown nipples,
panting caught on film.

A form letter arrives
bearing oranges and pears sent
from a place in the sun,
fungus halted by sterile note,
a mail order gift,
non-poison fruit
you will lick with your tongue,
watching for lumps with your lips,
tasting again my fresh flesh.

Pregnant with Poems

Powder dusts moonsilver
temples that ache.
She twists
a thin tube of lipstick.
Fuchsia edged
her voice spills,
melts the heavy hand
laid on her thigh.
Her child poem
drops its head,
dilates her mind,
urges her to lay back,
spread her legs,
and push
through lips that rupture
cherry blossom bones.

Hormonal Injustice

A flash of sweat
corrodes my brow, my upper lip,
dampens neck, chest and back.
My head goes light
and desire leers naked –
to strip myself of heat.

I have bled through many sweats –
now I sweat an end to blood,
bright red erasing itself
in a nest of duck eggs.
Bosomed moon to moon
they hatch in tall grass
from the heat of down.

Moon to moon
I followed that cycle,
cleansed and recleansed.
Now I bleed sweat,
brooding in cycles of hot and cold
for shells, beak broken,
and the moon ovum
laid whole against the night sky.

Eclipse

When two moons rise
over the jaded hills
their lamp light dims
the passion
night hunt of dogs
who woo the mistress goose,
her shells laid
on stains straw damp.

Crows sit   black
beads on pumpkins.
Coyotes bay.
The shadowed sun girdles
their goose   mistress
in night's brown nod,
her blood feathers
gutted clean to wing,
her egg youth bitten
by dark eclipse.

Performance Zero Boy
at the Neurodose Cyberpunk Revue '92

Silver-suited futuristic Fly,
webs spun on a backdrop of light,
projected imaginary visions
behind psychedelic fractured repetitions
of Z Z Z Zero Boy.
Dressed in black neon,
he wakes in a computer coffee world,
bounces through mimed morning movements,
a roller ball in a flipper paddle arcade game,
catches a commuter subway
to a clockwork catechism routine.
Buzz words of sexual innuendo
shoot from behind the cover of a water cooler
at the stream-lined jet black woman.
Ah, but Zero Boy,
do not think you can work unseen
by Fly's silver slanted eyes.
Gender bender —
she somersault flips your awkward ego
into that pearly black purely feminine body,
pinched and squeezed,
high-heeled and stumbling
like a pugnacious scarecrow on stilts.
Your litany of confused grunts
will tell you what you did not believe.
And when Fly sees
your foundling vision of female funk
is righteously endorsed,
she flips you forward
into the web of the spider woman,
into a dark dementia of time and space,
devoid of toxic waste
except for your own thoughts,
vegetable progenerations seeded
by Sunday ministers and technician politicians.
Did you think your freedom flies

on the head of a bald eagle?
Spider woman's web is the fine line
between earth and air.
You can climb everywhere from there,
entangled in time,
and her bite,
her neurodose chemical poison,
will bring your bloodless cyberbrain to life.

Spider Woman

Spider white woman
blows discordant strings,
her jagged jazz harp billows the wind.
Webweaver catches light fire,
forests of dreaming.
Dew frozen crystals
touch ground against hard.

I brush away this webacross
with wind-broken branch.
White web
mother web
hangs in morning wet light,
sticky mock of maple sap
spilled raw.

By day she mends arhythmic.
At night her full moon rises,
gnats and flies wound tight
string from her pouch.
She bites the flagging wind,
reeds vibrate her teeth.

I stumble
chirping cricket notes.
She wraps me in white,
covers my face with her cloth.
She eats the brown spill
of my fern spore.

Red Wood

Bulldozers crack the horizon.
Nested young heavy layered beneath brush
explode in motors of saws,
in wood chained bark
and ringwounded snags,
the hedge-tangled bone ache of maple and fir.
A cold sun sheds bitter hail,
pine scent shrouds the air.

Rain-spread fingers ply me
from this dark afternoon.
On the road to Hobart
a clear cut yokes my hope.
Shoulders welted from thorn,
I walk rock rubble and weeds
where spinal bones gone from meat
graft the once forest floor.

Cloven hooves dent the soil,
turn under splinters bladed from circular scars.
Seeds sunburnt naked against loam
stir fireweed's magenta ghosts.

Online
For Yitzak Rabin and Ken Saro-Wiwa

My memory is full
cross-wired to coexist
cross-continent
cross-colour-coded doc.s
the hard wear of skin.

Skinhead hackers
with scarred lips
lock up my keyboard,
crash my drive.
They modem lead hate
in binary word bytes.
Their graphic macros
curse cross-pollination,
embed files corrupted,
access denied.

With the click of a key
their virus enters the net.

The Silences

Politicos char my throb-to-know.
They lie under sheets of silence
after the panting stops.
My head nags
silence buried   unmarked
by grave disciples
after the telecast,
after the camera shuts off.

To say there is silence
after the storm
betrays silence swollen
in a battered black eye,
betrays silence   subcutaneous
in radioactive dens,
betrays the last breath
of the extinct.

Silence trickles down page gutters.
It pools at the end of a line.
Long and slow I fill
with tide whispered whole note,
its seismic rattle,
its sweat scent
breaks over me,
my skin leathery
silence unwound.

Sand Dune Walkers
After a photo by Edward Weston, *Dunes, Oceano,* 1936

Dune walkers climb ripple carved sand
shackled by wind.
Broken against the blue black night
they climb, they fall, they crawl
hands blistered,
knees bent
against the down drop sand.

They came
night air mosquito thick,
journeying through wounds bleeding
with piñon and pine scrub
away from tall building night life,
blue time sign clocking their stay.

Neon thorns cut their scalps.
In crown throb sweet wet
they came,
came to climb the desert high,
saguaros touching moon
bent to sweeping sand.

Porous drains mean
through burned feet
and with loins on fire
they walk naked into thorn trees.
An eclipse darkens the sky
with their heat scream.
Purified and sun-baked
they pry their escape,
red eyes blooming dusk.

Tin Soldiers

                    rust the lawn.
Tin feet bend the blades they march on
blades and bravado clenched in their teeth.
Tin guns armor chests painted
a crouch of blue
a crouch of green
a breath of blood shed in the same red way.
Morning tears open the sky
wipes its tears in cloud thunder.

Buried in black, the vet knuckles my table
with machine gun rap. *In Cambodia*
he says *I was sharp and fast*
one shot could kill
see my hands
his hand to mine
see how long   and quick
he jabs at spent matches
and my eyes   he squints
do you know?
what colour are my eyes?
his eyes open hard and   *blue!*
he shouts
in the dark   in Cambodia
I could see the mole on your neck
one shot could kill.

Shadows cross his tin eyes
his tin heart torn
his bones broken
buried in black hills.
Hills of black crosses
silhouette the night.
Young boys rust blood
skeletons silver the lawn.

Harvest Moon
The Hot Edge of Night

Turtle Moon paddles the night sky
catching seeds in her mouth.
She carries them moonbelly to Sun.
Sun floods her shell
and seed roots crawl in her turtle soil.

    Moon-swallowed,
    I emerge Corn Husk Woman
    to people the east of her ridged back.

Moon bares her turtle brass face,
lays her seed eggs in sand.
Seeds become trees,
trees flower, flowers plum,
plums purple her west brown shore.

    Plum Woman ripens.
    Jealous, I crawl out looking for rock.
    Sharp prayers split my tongue.
    I am Maize, seed oil suckled from soil,
    flesh kernels bitten with brass.
    Plum Woman dances, dark fingered
    husking eagle feather smoke.

My gold-eyed father raises his severing blade,
anoints my corn silk hair.
Plumblood scents Moon's beaded nose.
Fire chips fall from her face.

Mount St. Helens and Moss

Bleed the waiting women
into moss
their sacred time
their secret absorbent flame
seeded to earth.

This house
this waiting house
       too sacred.
Men cannot come
where women bleed
into the holy earthgrail
into moss pads
at one time
under one moon.

Mt. St. Helens cramps,
red drops bleed into moon.
Her belly caves.
Hot ash breaks her jaw
melting whiskers of trees.
Columbia drains
tears
boiled over with snow.
Ashen voice
dust blanket
curls around children
she bears on her skin.
She bleeds into moss
hot lava
her sacred waiting ground.

Dream Chase

A rosewood morn washed
in roan horse fog.
My balcony overlooks
wave rhythm.
A bear paddles white
through the slap of white surf.

From ocean through fog
he enters my room,
attacks my black horse,
claws streak
long red slices
into breast flesh,
horse wild hooves fly,
bear fangs flash,
the neighing growls,
sclera-eyed horse screams.

I follow
thickening blood,
scarlet noise
lost in halls of maize.
Bear meat angered,
my black horse dying,
a zebra stumbles
under tiger stripes.

I float in brine,
alone with words,
the fragrance of rose.
A hundred hummer bees
pollinate sumac.

When Horses Lame Beyond Repair
For Retortion

Black pony, my airborne drifter,
a jockey canes your sides
for long jumps and feather flight.
Rising with nods and shakes,
with slab broken bones,
you gather your crooked strength
and carry the wind on your back.

On a turn banked for speed
your knee cracks
and I feel your hard breath.
Heartquake triggers tsunami
and my mind floods
with soldier horses beating down grass.
Hot lead bites your flanks
and fire eats your flesh curves,
haunches and bone
dust ashens my face.

I have buried the bones of cats and geese.
Beneath lilac, their white skulls bloom,
parched reminders the dead give back.
Horse bones churn in memory's vat.

Purple Stains

There is always grape jelly
we wash from our lives.
The purple stain it leaves
reminds us of quiet mistakes
made in small rooms
at the ends of dark alleys.

Virginity spilled from me
after the prom,
a purple stain
on a mattress
in the furniture factory
where my young love worked.

I bled scared days,
tantalized
by the thought of pregnancy.
I wondered if Mother noticed
the time was not right.

Purple does not blend into freckled skin,
a foam mattress,
or a blonde young man turned grey.
Sweet stains
fall in my lap.

Bone Memory

I handled love the way I handled you,
grey goose.
Your broken back,
swollen hot throb, caressed my hand.
Flapping, you fell,
your once regal wings splayed the ground.

When you lay breath still
I tender towel wrapped your face,
but your struggle weakened my grip.
Fragile hours passed belly flat
before death gathered you.

On this day when I uproot fifteen years,
on this day when I dig through attic compost,
boxing old clothes, books and dust,
burying moldy leather and letters,
my shovel cracks the edge of your beak.
On this day when my blade finds its mark
I remember love's broken back.

My Brother's Dream Catcher Eyes

The wind tears pieces of skin
from a path where the hot mouthed flame
gorges the wooded shawl.

My dream blisters, ragged skin
catches your eyes, sinew laced
on the rocky shore.
Eagle feathers molt
our kayak in your wet
dream catcher.

From your little boy bed,
blonde hair blizzards and eye storms
of blue fractured I want yous
entangled my twelve-year-old
firstred piercing my lips
hormone heavy desire
for you, my surrogate son.

A beaver skull, its dense
bone empty sockets
and long orange teeth,
devours your pale flesh,
your wood meat swallowed.
Your underbelly dissolves in my blood.

Brother, I float cross-woven
in eyes tied with knots
we taught each other to hide.

Trilogy to Loss at the End of the Millennium

I. Leather, Lace, Tattoos & Attitude
An elegy for Heather McKay (1978 - 1997)

Tuning fork, your single pitch
holds its tone in hiway howl;
your throat open,
you sing beyond concrete barriers,
asphalt & truck metal.
Your song does not end
where medians flower with crabgrass.

Chanticleer at high noon,
the devil damps your tongs,
your pure note; his rage squeals,
four lanes raked by bumper steel.
Your song does not end
where a hubcap circles & falls,
repeating & repeating.

Heather, your song does not end
in a flat line sforzando
when breath surrenders.
Leather & lace vibrate.
Your tines ring my crystal edge.

Title from an album cover mock-up
by Heather McKay

II. To a Friend Diagnosed with Breast Cancer
New Year's Eve, 1997

In a tumbler of sluice water
we polish each other smooth.
Flesh opal and turquoise

rub amber cheekbones.
My rutiles stain your quartz
and your hand paints
its landscape on my picture agate.

Words   cancer and chemo
tumble between us.
Their waxed eyes roll.
Their rock shoulders bump
acid pearls and hematite jags
against your jade.
I did not count on the hardness of stone.

I cannot share
the knife across your chest,
the flush of your blood
through veins of iron.
Far from your molten core,
I cannot flow in your heat.
With pen, hammer tipped,
I can only chip with Saxon claws
at the syllables of your disease.

III. On the Fields of Rugby
  For John Robert LaDuca (1979 - 1998)

Water bleeds from my face,
spring tainted by winter's loss.
Crocus and daffodil telescope
green spines out of pithy bulbs,
branches sprout what you cannot.

With blithe hand you wrapped the cord
that leaves us hung above a field
where dandelions do not yet tilt.
What private scrum entangled you,
your fragile seed a puff of white?

Was your root so shallow,
so easily plucked
by clouds' cumulus mounds?

Your well-placed knot sealed our loss.
Did you reckon your final play
would leave us paupers in winter
without the coat of your smile,
naked in a wind of bitter blades?

Beach Prayer

Praying like a motherfucker
I kneel in gravel,
beach sea bed,
washed up storms.
I lean over,
cup seablue crystals,
pure baptismal memory splashed
on a white clad babe
by the hand of god presumed.
I kneel on gravel
self-splashed,
self-healed,
self-baptized
against storms   brutal
the laugh of gulls,
angels above my head.

A motherfucker on knees
praying,
the uneven crunch of stones
smooth and round slide away.
I move further down
into kelp and eel grass,
their stain breaches
the seasong wail
of orcas and otters.
Dead jellyfish slime
the in and out surf,
the callous tide
leaves and returns
used condoms and coke cans,
the unholy worshipped holy,
the prayers of a motherfucker
left cold.

I Want to Bloom

Tumbling from the basket hung
my life pours green.
Fuchsia breasts open milk white hearts.
I summer endless deadhead days.

Wilted blossoms let go their soft handhold
and fall,
nectar stripped by humming
birds hover bowing fronds.

Teardrops of fruit refused,
pods picked fat with seed
force new blooms
I feed with fertile water stream
pushing life and life
in slow arms before fall's cold
sleeps in my veins.

Nailed
to the
Sky

Crossing Thresholds

Ducks arabesque through lily pads
and geese thrub wing overhead.
My black silhouette paddles
the sound zippered with sun
crossing thresholds.

I have flame-tangled lightning-set words
and spat them out,
fragile pennings that burn my fingers.
Smoke stains my eyes.
Salt fire, holy water fire,
I tong words in the spitting light,
in tongues lapping yellow and red,
and the dog moon wets my skin.

Alabaster currents drag me
on shelves of purple and black.
A finger with its nail on fire
pushes the small of my back.
Word eel wraps around me,
curls and darts me
deeper into ship's wreckage.

The word licks her finger, touches my forehead,
licks her finger, touches my heart,
touches each shoulder, then bows.
I turn transparent
and paper becomes wet.
She has seared herself into my white skin.
I am word child
flowing blue
mingling with ocean currents
and flame has eaten me up.

On paper, thrown into forge fire
I am hardened to steel,
welded with ink.

Nails driven into my arms
hold me to the foot of the she-wild-word
who pushes through water skin
sounding for air.
On paper's burning edge
word suns drop,
green flash before dark.

Riding the Mirage

Your *sumi-e* horse hangs on my wall,
you the artist   I blending
ink and gold to a magazine cover,
we bend over, head to head,
each overlay precise,
brush strokes fluid and spare.

> Haze wavered,
> the hot horizon siphons me,
> its glare wicks my lips.

Who knew your cancer would come between us,
that your flow would stop
in the prick of nausea and nightly hot flashes,
that steel would stroke your chest?

> The clock sun ticks.
> Tar pools from asphalt melt,
> lizards squat with tongues outstretched.
> Cattle and dusk surround me.

More than a year has passed
since haze covered your eyes.
Your sisters   blood   attended you.
I stayed away.
The gold in our manes faded.

> Hides brush me with brown,
> nudge me herd center,
> shadow milling shadow,
> a wicket of bone on bone.

I said I was angry.
You would not speak.
You said you were angry
and still would not speak.

Cowboys on horses drive us,
dogs nip at our heels.
Bound by rustlers and tar pits
we bawl in the uneasy sand,
feet roiling the steel-blue heat.

I said I was angry   yes –
at blood   dust
the trail you rode.
You said you were angry
I was not there.

Your ruby soprano slices the air.
It leads me beyond thorn pillars,
beyond cowponies' nicker and neigh,
out of rawhide's haze.

Sumi-e Horse

Still
white head
wind-flagged by mane and tail
lungs deep-caged and breath heavy
legs fire forward
race white paper away from frame
onto a sand track.
Canary yellow silks
kneel into saddle silence
above tornado brown
a storm cantered
across long ago desert drifts
now whirls grandstand benched crowds
cheers and faces sucked into his path
my windthought sucked in
where my eyes kneel
centered
in the Zen silent
white head.

Boundaries

My rottweiler lines the fence,
scent droppings
press against the weight
of the dog that pees outside
pressing back.

I line pots along the drive,
mow exact short grass,
scatter seed,
my soul scent fragrant
in rose, carnation and marigold.

The neighbor   north
leaves her mark with child screams,
cold Christs on the sill,
and a look that comes on to me
when her loose pup tramples St. Johnswort.
Goddamn leans heavy on my rake
scraping the scent
she, nose deaf,
should smell with her eyes.

Fenced in pyracantha
and Lake Washington kelp,
my neighbors   south
welcome me with flame –
trout grilled over mesquite,
chardonnay heating leaf
mulch piled against winter's chill.

Through lilac's lavender sign
we watch red frilled tulips open,
troll for words
from a boat of overturned rocks,
rub jowls, like cats,
lip wet with scent.

Moving, 1996

Snow blocks the road.
My old dog stumbles down
powder white steps
using my leg for balance,
I, rail held and afraid,
my bad back covered in sleet.

Icy nails remind me,
this house has private parts
written by another's hand,
painted in wide brush strokes,
trimmed with lattice
and floral wall prints.

She has left her pain
in the thin air resting between tiles
where grout cracks away,
in small holes punched
by door knobs slammed against walls,
locked against her own healing,
left to me with unmarked keys
and sticky door jambs.

I close her open windows
against flies and the muscovy
that would roost in the downstairs bath.
I open and close her cupboard yawns,
make the bed,
take down the curtain
she used to haze the view.

A limb of flowering plum,
wet heavy with white,
breaks and falls
as I enter the drive.
It is mine now.
I feel its weight
tender the ground.

Moving, 1997

I dig iris from beds,
surprised at the clutch
of their trollish tubers.
Upheaval urged by sale of house,
I wrench their clenched fingers
from soil my crone claws did not sink into,
my roots shallow among rose horns.
Mountain ash and maple push at the fence.
Verbena swallows the porch
the willow corkscrew cracks.

Autumn draws in its yeast breath.
I move to orange water reflected in fireglass.
In the crook of a rock wall
I bed down tubers,
iris and claws loam woven,
crone cloth knit by muscovies.
Goose dawn hisses,
cats meow.
Their tenor soprano tells me I'm home.

Waterland Festival and Fireworks
Des Moines, 1996

Puget Sound laps at my edge.
Crystal daylight shatters,
watershards tangled
with wood drift and wine.
Sun silver drops behind ridge,
its quick slide into black
measured in cork screw turns.

Bottled inside this night,
inside octopus arms
split by carnival lights,
the butter taste of oak
presses the glass green sky.
Pavement's breath belly distends.

Chrysanthemums and buzz bombs
hammer my heart,
hummer shells belch their spit hiss.
Their two-fold bloom
spirals into my flesh soft cork.

A deepening twist tugs me
from gill nets' loose hold,
unhands my throat
and exposes my amber to air.

Reverie
**On moving from the WTBA Sales Pavilion at
Longacres Race Track to the Morris J. Alhadeff Sales
Pavilion at Emerald Downs**

Fifty years of thunder lump in our throats.
Acres long on grief, we squeeze no more tears.
A single heron blue among reeds gulps silver darts.
Cattails explode, each seed the float of man and mount.
Season to season, I know hawk's territorial cry,
coyote's lair hidden in field grass,
the path of wild geese.

After twenty years, my ground shifts.
Trains rumble body and heart.
I do not see heron or hawk
or hear coyote's bounding bark.
I do not know if the mallard will find its mate.

From a valley of dark clouds
the screams of sale horses echo new.
Auction shouts this vaulted roof with white heat,
this podium unmarked by calligraphy of hoof.

Rainier's white pinnacle rises,
a holy ghost at the altar where we offer
hoof thunder, the steam of sweat on flesh,
the harangue of gate metal, the crescendo crowd,
pinned ears, huffing snorts,
the circling of hot walkers.

Daybreak rustles in stalls,
nickers rising to anxious whinnies,
then grain-muzzling silence.
A pair of mallards silhouette the emerald sky.

Breath Wind

The wicked cement tears paper and flesh.
My feet, dog-old, walk the remains of ash,
ankles torn chainrub raw.
A gull picks at littered wrappers and gum,
my guiltbound blood.
Its cry gut raids my hollow.

Outside city walls,
a harrier shifting wing weight
hovers prey empty fields.
Naked air touches my tattered raw,
odor blind and begging for fill.
Then his breath,
stronger than gravity's iron will,
lifts me on currents of hawksoar wind.

Gathering Herbs

Earth's damp hand reaches
through denim and wets my knees.
I part leafy sage, finger tips
stirring flavour scent from green bellies.
Oregano tucks its shoulder
into dill's unshaven pit,
nudging breast smooth tips
against course parsley's chest.
Rosemary fronds stroke
the pelvic curve of marjoram,
the long slow curl of tarragon,
leggy tendrils of thyme.
Scissor blades coax grave offerings
from lemon balm and lavender,
purple basil's blood scent.
Tomato, fruit virgin,
hangs heavy with wait.

After Reading *The Autobiography of Malcolm X*

When big dogs fight
black and tan torn
by white tooth
next to embers low
the once fire dying
under sky black
stars thrown out
the scattering
of bird crumbs
hiss the evergreen boughs
laid on coals hot
and the black dogs growl
the one humbled
the other's Spartan dew
collects on rock.

Franciscan monk
black and tan
swallows the dew from
white toothed Christian mothers
who taught we are
brothers born from the same bitch
or not at all
Taught
night cries outside the convent wall
are wolves after scraps
thrown out to keep them at bay
Dawn he looked
for prints
their near thrill danger
dissolved under villagers
who walked the night.

The lying hearts of motherguiders
taught what they believed
the choke right catechisms
the separate ceremonies

the caring pretended at him
His boxed ears
deadened the growling silent
the question in his eyes
The followed rituals
the words said right
the meantnothing words
said right
kept the outside wolves at bay
the hunger they chewed
white punctured holes
A growl lows its way up.

The big dogs growled —
it was Christ
Christ spoke —
it was Buddha
Buddha spoke —
it was Allah
Allah spoke —
and the wolves outside
were in him
were him
humbled all that he knows.

The Unfound Door
"looking for a stone, a leaf, an unfound door."
– From *Autobiography,* by Lawrence Ferlinghetti

A preacher in jeans first served me God
black in coffeehouse dregs
with parodies of Ferlinghetti.
You must find the door,
walk naked into the cold,
bare your sins, flog your shearling skin
and praise the wool woven warmth He gives.

In the shadow of bell hollows
my goat throat bahs Allah.
Prism trees chrome the crooked path.
I kneel, my forehead touching east.
Yahweh snuffs my hair, my clothes.
Nostril to nostril we gather scent.

In lupine and salmonberries
I nibble nettle fruit.
Jehovah's thorn stings my side.
Through brambles I follow a she-goat.
She hides from me, her small hooves
cut trails narrow and false.

In a clearing,
at a table empty and wide,
God leans full weight before me.
He reads me rhymes of menued verse.
He drinks deli dregs,
my blood steamed in a wax paper cup.
His mustard cuts my breath.

Across threshold uneven rock,
Buddha buds in lotus lilies.
I wade his crib shallow riverbed.
In pond cress walking on water
I flower, pollen tufted,
and rub the legs of bees.

Hendrix Sings the Blues
For J.R.

Earphones jacked to a small black box,
I think you are radioed in to baseball
or news-rovered to Mars.
Word and note,
house finch and chickadee
flitter outside your glass pane.
They peck at your siren seed.

Beethoven, beat of the nineties,
you have penned coyote counterpoint,
evangelical lute breathing fire and snake,
Beckett and Escher boiled
with Christ on your tongue.
Now you hold sound in your hand
as you held me,
my virgin dam broken in blood
spawned streams
and words Mozart teased into chords.

Soundslides fill your ears with flies,
but mind music straddles purple haze —
you still hear sweet and sour
in the buzz of phrase-broken silences
and you still remember Jimi.

A Poet at a Poetry Reading
on the Poet's Birthday
For I. D.

Readin' poems,
hearin' poems,
we all bein' poems
while the black woman sings.
Oh baby, she sings,
while I feel straight-jacket white,
straight jacket
like the symphony conductor
who says he doesn't want to be here.
She wants him to feel
the word,
the music,
the beat,
and he says she took him somewhere
he doesn't want to be?
Somewhere he doesn't want to be,
and I'm like
take me further, baby, take me all the way,
unlock my white
and take me.

Sometimes No Return
From a dream

There is no return.
I lowered myself
down three sink drains
with dental floss for rope.
One after another I went
lower
and lower
until the third washed me
uncontrolled
away
into a station hall
where men wait on mats.
Not knowing, they wait
and when I arrive
fresh
and female
they make me their leader.

I was not looking for new kingdoms.
But here —
queendom
and a thousand men on blue mats
at the bottom of a drain.

Breakfast in Bremerton

> Leaving the ferry, the pier touches my ass
> with tight fingers, pinches my coral belief
> that gender reef keeps us apart.

We settle into a saloon with breakfast specials
for a buck to three ninety-five.
The waitress takes our order —
two for steak and eggs, two for bacon
and our choice of wheat or white.
A jellyfish flowing tendril arms,
she floats away and you ask
What do you call that look?
That wild woman look,
the biker chick big hair cut in a shag look,
the big-bosomed poster girl in western duds look?
And do they wear Wonderbras?

> Barriers reef us awake in our bedroom at dawn,
> you with your hard-on and me with my hunger
> that screams I want you.

We are bacon and egg voyeurs
to the steak you order rare.
Crunching coral we tell all
about underwire support, false cleavage
and hair curled carefully carefree.
Why do they do it? you ask
watching the tight jeans, small waist and longs legs
bring silverware to our table and drinks to the bar.

> I shift in my chair, the memory
> of your dawn fingers in the curls of my soft furlings,
> my hollow hunger stinging the bare skin of our love.

No, I don't own a Wonderbra.
Good, you say, I'm proud of you,
I like my steak grey.

I haven't watched a tight boy butt
in months, she says. I know she has.
The dude toes up to the line in muscled jeans.
She twists her napkin into a long tight cord
she moves back and forth in her hand.
He throws his dart, she licks her lips
and another coral branch breaks.
The waitress serves our meals
with sea salt and brine.
We eat in silence and heavy breathing.

    Anemone clinging to black rock coral
    my tentacles brighten to red,
    dangle bait and wait for your bite.

Mozart Piano Quartet

Cello, violin, viola
spread my pores,
piano pulses
the heart beat
rhythm that bursts
as logs on fire.
I burn,
breathe the smoke
of four men bowing,
bodies bent instrumental.

Four men thrust and heave
the fiery way men move
when they mount their women,
weave their love
with strings and ivory
pushing away the sheets.
I watch them spew
the milky cream
of clustered chords,
writhing pauses
over breasts hard
in the wash of viola.

Dazed
I guard against
the wild slipping in my mind
off their hands,
the wild I dare not touch.
Fire banked,
the curtain drops.
Spent and sticky
I stand, beating my palms,
the taste of warm fish on my tongue.

Cello Suite

The wind is my father
a bull elephant in musth,
my mother a cello
her belly full
her refrain   a choral chord.
His hairs rub her strings
his bellows inflate her lullabies.

She does not bend
where his hand touches her neck
where his legs wrap her curves
his knee in her side.
He presses her heart
major and minor
tremourous frets stop her strings
for the note he bows.
His breath is the wind she yawns
his wide arm in flight is the white crane
that picks gnats from her back.
And she,
she is the wood resonance
for his vibrato.

Ouroboros
For my maternal grandmother

She walks catacomb paths,
her feet sandaled,
her greyblack hair unpinned.
Rivers cover her breasts
sapphire they leak when I cry.

Beneath stone horizons,
down stone cambered steps,
she points to a litany scribed
in a stone wall.
Her lips mouth the dark.
Her ink negra nib
tattoos glyphs on my blank papyrus.

Vultures shadow the corridor.
Serpents fly from her hair.
They lead me
past chamber runes,
her incense on wing,
her shaft steep and stepless.
My hand brailles her wall.

She is the serpent Nile.
She swallows her daughter.
Her daughter, the black sand,
carries my salt in her arms.
She swallows me
and I swallow
salt and sand and the serpent sea.
Fluid, I flow through their gate.

Bird of Soul
My Brother's Song

Baby blue in tux, he took our sister's arm.
He waltzed her prom,
her romance high on pain;
his alto song, a chorus
of sax and electric high notes.

With me on the road to New Mexico
he traced our roots on a map,
his song a single line;
his breath a whole note held
between my screaming guitars,
volume pouring blood,
when a detour lost our way.

Ford Fairlane overhot in a Gallup garage,
endstopped
at a countrywestern motel,
we smiled at a rednecked cowboy in black,
white Cadillac flagged out in U.S. blues.

Now, in the low light of a Portland café,
I see a bar of our father's song
phrased in my brother's eyes,
song and variations,
earth scales, lichen-thin,
scribed on rock's raw face,
a host of hallelujahs.

The Sixth Gate

My birth exit,
first canal purging my mother's soil,
opened five times more,
each time new carving a spine in her delta fan.
The sixth, her water son,
mingles Aleutian, Gulf, Atlantic.
He holds his breath in her womb salt.

Brother, in the flight path of dream
you land at a gate I can't find.
Over loud speakers you call me to come.
You call   *What is my name?*
Where I go is unknown.

I worm a path, circular hallway,
past gate number three,
past a heavy-set man who whines
he must eat before flight,
past gate number four,
dreadlocks in pair,
past gate number five
where lovers' fingers silk the arm
of man on man, their restless wrestle
pushing head to hip.

Your plane crosses my sun,
its dark startle,
a moose unending in cloud.
I find you on a tarmac
of blue sapphires waking,
antlers strung with worms
you shake from my heart,
your harp teasing the tonal wind.

Brother Atlantic, we grew
anaerobic in subsoil.
Follow my exit —

drop your head,
burrow out when it rains.
I will shed my red vest
and hand you my down.

Handmade Paper
Folklife Festival, 1993

Sister I and Brother
wander
the people thick pulp,
notes, leaves, petals of flower children,
stirred
bits in pulpish lines.
Sharp-eyed vendors call
crowds teased into touching
their belly-fill wants.
Rose petals
surface
when currents change,
the fire green blue way two little girls
spin
their red head flower garlands
mix
with short dresses
tight shorts
the side-eyed glance
dance of young women
a middle-age mama
massaged by her man.

Scooped
into pan pipes
and drum dreams,
we pour ourselves down,
sponge
off our excess,
two white squares
papered.

Intertribal

Coyote braves yip
the red rhythm of ankle bells.
Drum hearts thunder,
my chest percussed
by mallet and mansong.
Squash blossoms silver my breast.
Dress jingles, feather fans and I
dance the bark of trees tangled in cloud.

A wasp circles my skin, white petals,
the pollen scent of my hair.
Its sting is the wild peyote.
Its wing buzz this vision –

> A white bear bites off the head
> of a salmon for its fish gold eyes,
> throwing the body, silver bait
> into the cold sea.

I cover my blonde with the shawl wind,
turn, unturn,
drink the salt I have mined.

Kachina

I squat beside a blanket laid out with silver and beads.
The ratchet laugh of a roadrunner cackles,
The kiln is cold and the knife still.

I am Raven Boy.
Adobe mother molded me, water and soil.
Raven carved my mask with his beak.
He taught the turquoise to talk,
led my fingers to listen,
obsidian and coral inlaid in dreams.

Sweat casts my temples in veins of lead.
Machine heat shapes my heart,
sky blue and silicone-sealed,
shelled against the aging oil,
against the touchrub darking it to aqua.

Buffalo lick me,
their tender tongues tell me
Go back to the fire
that burned away your straw mold,
that left you bare and buried in sand.

Raw ore shafts my heart,
agate and flint fall at my feet.
I climb back into clay.
I am turquoise, heat and lead.
I am Raven flying through canyons of sand.

Ripple

Bricks fired under the raven sun
stacked block on block
fill my night with wind whistles.
I lie among curled tails of scorpions,
my back against a cave shell
carved in sunset stone.

Smoke rises where saguaros burn.
A scorpion offers me the red pipe of his tail.
I inhale   his clay on my lips,
his poison leads me to the precipice.
The wind blows my hair
but cannot turn my feet.
I am Oyster Woman,
a single grain of sand
overlooking a tidal flow of dunes.

An eagle soars.
He calls to me
Oyster Woman, Monarch Butterfly,
open your oval wings.
Migrate with me to a river of chum.
Lay your sand seed with the salmon's roe,
redden the stream with our spawn.
When their quills sprout,
white heads and gold wings,
they will swim the blue adobe wind,
follow the scent of saguaro smoke
and curl in a bed of scorpion tails.

Sangre de Cristo

3 a.m.
Jasper colours New Mexico hills.
I am sober now.

I did not come here to rise from the dead,
but sage scratched my arms,
sign of a telltale fervor
led by peyote buttons
onto the red hills at sunset.
I ate the desert chill.

Pineapple sherbet curdled around
dirt brown peyote — my belly warmed
with Christ in my gut.
I firewalked across rock
desert hot in the midnight sun.

I became Christ.
Water became wine.
The vinegar hallelujahs,
shouts of Sangre de Cristo,
the meltwant feel —
I am red sand bled
from the veins of piñon trees.
I am Crow nailed to the sky.

To the Poet Anna Akhmatova

Poetess –
this she-word haunts
like lights that chase on a freeway at night.
A seamstress sewing sentences,
it snivels,
like adulteress or victress.
It sticks in my throat,
cold French fries,
stale rites.

I build word stones,
a fortress,
and lay my breast on its wall,
sheltered from the hiss of snakes.
They spit esses,
their venom numbs my lips.

In estuaries,
mud flats suck my booted feet,
arthritic esses climb my wall.
Enwombed, they hissper
waitress   mistress   songstress   poetess.

Out of labour's thunder
I birth blue,
the sky trailing star silver.
Laughing, I shout out *goddess.*

photo by Chuck Smart

Poet and artist M. Anne Sweet was born in Albuquerque, New Mexico, first of six children. Sweet and her family moved frequently within the western United States, Canada and then Alaska. She returned to Albuquerque to study art, art history and literature at the University of New Mexico. Since the mid-seventies she has resided near Seattle, Washington, working as the art director for *Washington Thoroughbred* magazine. She continues to hone her poetic craft through interaction with other writers and artists and is currently collaborating with three percussionists, combining improvisational music and poetry.